CW01081109

THE CONC
TO DIOR

The Rise to Fame and
Remarkable Story of One of
Fashion Powerhouse(Small
Manual of Fashion 1)

Cipriano Fanucci

TABLE OF CONTENT

CHAPTER 1

INTRODUCTION

Dior is a Paris-based fashion brand that has become a household name across the world. As soon as it was founded, it had a profound effect on the fashion business. Although it's popular and conventional, its reputation as a top-tier designer of high-end couture continues to get stronger. Dior's ready-to-wear stylish leather products and accessories, as well as its footwear, have revolutionized the fashion industry. Known as a prominent fashion industry player for more than seven decades, the firm is a household name in the fashion sector. Millions of people's lives have been influenced by Christian Dior's legendary brand thanks to his creative mind.

CHAPTER 2

What was the identity of Christian Dior?

His name is Christian Dior, and he was born on this date one hundred ninety-five years ago today in Paris, France. Dior's first spring/summer 1947 collection was unveiled on February 12th. Carmel Snow, Editor-in-Chief of Harper's Bazaar, was convinced of Dior's abilities after seeing his initial success. "My dear Christian, you're witnessing a major shift! Your clothes have taken on a completely different look, if that makes any sense." She let out a loud scream. Thus, a new fashion trend was born, and the "New Look" became a trademark. With its distinctive and inventive shapes such as shorter, fuller skirts and tightened waistlines among other things, Dior's items were groundbreaking when they were first created in the 1940s. Being one of the most successful fashion designers in the world, he was well-known across the world for his creations and business practices. Celebrities and aristocracy alike have sported his designs, and his brand has been at the forefront of the fashion world ever since.

CHAPTER 3

The New Dior

After World War II, Paris had become a fashion mecca, and THE NEW LOOK by Dior was a huge success in bringing back Haute Couture. Dior's "The New Look" gowns had a narrow, nipped-in waist and a long, mid-calf-length skirt that accentuated an hourglass figure in contrast to the postwar period's more conservative outfits. Other designers were inspired by Dior's "Bar" suit from his 1947 debut collection and began incorporating it into their own collections.

For a long time before Christian Dior's meteoric rise in the fashion industry, he was known as an outlier who shunned social events and preferred to live alone in a remote location. Alexander Louis Maurice Dior, owner of a fertilizer company, and his wife, Isabelle, were the parents of the second of their five children. Christian Dior's family relocated to Paris, where he grew up. Because of this,

Dior's father encouraged him to pursue political science and convinced him to enroll in the École des Sciences Politiques in Paris to begin his studies.

With the aid of his father's financial and lending backing, he launched a modest art gallery in 1928. The agreement was that he wouldn't use the family name above the gallery entrance. Among the artists represented at Dior's gallery were Pablo Picasso, Georges Braque, Jean Cocteau, and Max Jacob. In 1931, he was forced to close the gallery because of the deaths of both his brother and mother. This happened at the same time that his father's company had a serious financial difficulty.

In 1940, he was drafted into the military and shifted his career path under the guidance of a well-known fashion designer, Robert Piguet. Dior was a French army commander stationed in the south of France.

After the German invasion of France in 1940, Christian Dior

returned to Paris and was employed by couturier Lucien Lelong. Aside from Dior and Pierre Balmain, he also made garments for Nazis and French collaborators, all in an effort to keep the fashion industry alive throughout the war for both commercial and artistic reasons.

The cotton-fabric magnate Marcel Boussac provided the financial backing for Christian to open his own fashion company on December 16, 1946, at 30 Avenue Montaigne in Paris. It is believed that Dior's initial summer and spring collections were shown in 1947, which is the year the house of Dior was founded.

Dior took a vacation in Italy's Tuscany region of Montecatini in 1957 after spending months on the cover of Time magazine. On October 23, 1957, he suffered his third heart attack and died at the age of 52, while traveling across the country. Yves Saint Laurent, who was to be his successor, was among the estimated 2,500 individuals who attended his funeral.

THE NAME OF THE GAME IS
DIOR.

Throughout the world, Dior's
work was praised for its
emphasis on highlighting and
elevating feminine bodies. To
honor the memory of one of his
sisters who was a member of
the French Resistance and
survived the Ravensbrück
detention camp, he launched his
first perfume in 1947.

Fashion for more than a decade
was defined by Dior's designs,

which remain one of the most striking trends to this day, a combination of classicism and modernism. Over time, the brand has developed into one of the world's best-known, best-recognized and best-loved fashion companies. Throughout its history, the House of Dior has built a reputation for using the best materials in its designs. At this time, Dior became a household name among the rich and famous, and he collaborated with Marilyn Monroe and Elizabeth Taylor.

To highlight Christian Dior's international development, the business opened a store in New York City in late 1949. Towards the end of the same year, Dior outfits alone accounted for about 75 percent of Paris' fashion exports and 5 percent of France's entire export revenue.

In 1949, Douglas Cox, a businessman from Melbourne, Australia, traveled to Paris and set up a meeting with Christian Dior in order to examine the possibility of having Dior designs created specifically for the

Australian market. In the next year, Christian Dior and Douglas Cox formed a contract in which Dior agreed to create unique designs for Douglas Cox to construct in his Flinders Lane factory.

CHAPTER 4

What exactly does Dior have to offer?

Dior, a well-known luxury brand, carries a wide range of products. The business has gained the trust of all of its clients, starting with its unique clothing line and proceeding to its well-known scents. It's no wonder that Dior products are sought after because of their amazing clothing and perfume lines. Other sections of the fashion industry have been added to Dior's product offering.

Cosmetics and skin care items manufactured by Dior may be found on the company's website, including those mentioned here.

Dior Skin's face makeup includes foundations, concealers, powders, blushes, and sun protection.

Mascara, eye shadow, eyeliner, and eyebrows are all types of eye makeup.

The Dior Addict collection
includes lipstick, gloss, lip
pencils, and lip balm (lip
cosmetics range).

There are two possibilities here:
manicures and nail lacquers.

Brushes and powders are two
examples of makeup
accessories.

In addition to cleanser, toner,
and face masks, face skincare
offers premium anti-aging and
international anti-aging
skincare. Included with this

treatment are wrinkle and stiffness corrections.

Cosmetics that keep the skin hydrated and refined

Specialized treatment for the eyes is called "eye care."

Self-tanners and sunblock are two types of sun care products.

Products for shaving, relaxation, healing, and nourishment are all part of men's grooming products.

Fashionable clothing for men and children is now part of the Dior clothing range, which was formerly just for women. With their rich, premium assortment of attractive bags, they have created a whole new fashion trend that is appreciated by women throughout the world.

It'd be amazing to discover how this business has survived and thrived since 1947 while also adapting to changes in the industry. Every new product from Dior has met or exceeded the company's rigorous quality requirements.

Dior celebrates his birthday today.

In addition to Yves Saint Laurent, Marc Bohan; Gianfranco Ferré; John Galliano; Raf Simons and Maria Grazia Chiuri, there have been six artistic directors who have taken over for Dior following his death. Fashions have evolved and developed in a different path for each of them. It is generally agreed that Saint Laurent was responsible for taking the brand into the twenty-first century, although Bohan has gone in a more conventional path, while Ferré has come up with ideas that are romantic and defined.

The Lady Dior handbag, designed and manufactured by Ferré, was a one-of-a-kind occasion for the Dior brand. For its rattan style, circular top handles, and gold charms, among other things, Princess Diana's tiny black leather grab bag was a huge hit.

A well-known and well-respected fashion house like Dior has a long history of creating stylish and amusing clothing for women of all ages. According to Dior's effort and aim to make women feel attractive, numerous well-known designers have replicated and drawn inspiration from Dior's sophisticated apparel range. Lady Dior's purse has become an icon in the eyes of many, including yourself.

CHAPTER 5

SUMMARY OF DIOR

Christian Dior has long been associated with feminine beauty and timeless flair in the fashion industry. As far back as the 1940s, this French fashion house has been making stunning clothing for ladies all over the world, whether they're cocktail party dresses or haute couture gowns for the red carpet that command the attention of everyone in attendance.

Dior's own brand has also lasted the test of time, evolving with each new generation of creative genius that has come through its doors. For many years, the fashion company has welcomed some of the best and brightest in the business, with more to come.

Discover the rich history of Christian Dior and how it came to be the renowned fashion house it is today.

Is there any information on how and where Christian Dior got his start?

As a result of its first collection being released in 1947, Christian Dior is regarded as having been formed in 1946, notwithstanding that fact. Christian Dior founded the company at 30 Avenue Montaigne. It took less than three months for Christian Dior's first collection to be created following the launch of the business on Feb. 12, 1947.

Before entering the fashion industry, Dior owned and maintained a gallery in France where he displayed his love of art. It was during the Great Depression that he was forced to close his gallery and subsequently moved on to work for fashion houses like Robert Piguet and Lucien Long. In spite of this, Christian Dior aspired to start his own fashion house, which is why he did so in 1946, naming it Christian Dior.

Christian Dior invented the term "New Look" during his very first

Paris presentation. When World War II came to an end, the collection was created to honor it with structural lines, nipped waists, and shorter billowy skirts to do so, reports Culture Trip. The gowns were opulent, averaging 20 yards of fabric each outfit. This fashion house quickly became one of the most wanted and admired on earth as a result of Christian Dior's innovations, which were revolutionary at the time.

Celebrities from Rita Hayworth to Margot Fonteyn sought out

Christian Dior's avant-garde New Look, which was decades ahead of its time, for their wardrobes. It's no wonder that the brand has expanded so quickly and become one of the most famous in fashion history because of the high-profile women who have worn his ensembles.

Expansion of Dior in New Markets

The name Christian Dior became a household one quickly. On Fifth Avenue and 57th Street in New York City, Christian Dior's first store in the United States opened its doors in 1948. A wider range was made available to coincide with the product's global debut. Scent was the starting point for Dior, who launched Miss Dior as a tribute to his sister. Also at this time, Dior realized that in order to retain his New Look, his business had to give the entire fashion experience from beginning to end. Essentially, this meant that the Dior name would be licensed for use in accessory manufacturing as well. This meant that the Christian Dior lady would now be free to adorn from head to toe with coats, shoes, and any other accessories she saw necessary to fully portray the New Look.

He dressed some of the most prominent people of the day and era, and his brand continued to grow. Even Marlene Dietrich's costume for Alfred Hitchcock's Stage Fright was done by him. She, along with a plethora of other Hollywood A-listers, relied on his designs throughout the late 1940s and early 1950s.

Yves Saint Laurent's first foray into the world of fashion design

He began his work with Christian Dior in 1955, when he was just 19 years old and had a youthful appearance. When he started working as Christian Dior's assistant, the young Frenchman quickly caught the eye of the designer. He reportedly told Saint Laurent's mother in 1957 that he had decided to hand over the family business to him when he stepped down from the fashion business. The fact that he was only 21 at the time was not a deterrent for Dior, who saw his talent for fashion and design.

After Christian Dior's death,

After a massive heart attack, Dior died in 1957. His death at the tender age of 52 rocked the fashion business, which was shocked to learn that a legend had died away so young. Following the death of Dior, Saint Laurent was named artistic director of the brand to ensure that the company would not deviate from its original path.

At the tender age of 21, the young designer maintained a

large portion of Dior's initial creative vision in his creations. By loosening their tight waistlines and allowing some of the structure to shine through, he tried to soften the brand's basic shape. Although it took a while, the fashion industry struggled to find a replacement for Yves Saint Laurent as the face of the Christian Dior brand after the latter was conscripted into military service in 1960.

Miss Dior is a Parisian fashion designer.

The first Dior fragrance, Miss Dior, was debuted in 1947 and is still in production today, despite its age.

Designers in France and Europe faced a moral dilemma during World War II, as the economy did not allow for the manufacturing of high-end luxury clothing. Fashion designer Lucien Long relied on Dior to keep his company alive during World War II by dressing the wives of Nazi leaders and French collaborators.

Catherine Dior, Dior's younger sister, was imprisoned in Ravensbruck concentration camp for her role in the French

Resistance at this time. When
she was liberated in 1945, her
brother Christian would devote
his first perfume to her as a
tribute to her strength and
tenacity. His extremely feminine
designs, according to legend,
were inspired by his sister's
strength and beauty.

THE END

Printed in Great Britain
by Amazon